I0020419

Live Smart

Be More Productive

Book Series

Mastering Microsoft Windows 10

The Most Powerful Windows Operating System Ever Made by
Microsoft Corporation

Written By

Eng. Mohanad Alablesh

ISBN: 1650570945

Contents

Letter from the Author

First of all, thanks for buying one of my book series that aim to develop the capacities of the current and the coming generations; from my opinion, most of the employees and service providers who work on Microsoft Windows 10, **don't know the power of this operating system and its built-in applications, that could solve most of the problems and issues needed at work**, without the need to look for other applications. Microsoft Corporation worked hardly for years to build most of the powerful applications in their operating system, just to increase the productivity and to make this operating system the most powerful one ever made by them. So, every employee must have this book at his desk ready for use when and where is needed. Having the knowledge on how to deal with the **most powerful**, **hidden** and **needy features** in our daily work routine, that are available in MS Windows 10, will help you a lot to give **qualitative** and **quantitative** work at the same time. In this book, I'll try to mention some of the most **powerful shortcuts** on the keyboard mostly available in windows 10 only. Even in this book, we will have a section about the **Personal Digital Assistant** called **Cortana** created by Microsoft Corporation, to be a real personal assistant for every one of us who is using MS Windows 10, and will have a section on how to go green with some options that **might save a tree** on our **lovely Earth**.

Productivity is one of the most important issues for every person who is giving a service or doing a job with a specific period of time, that might be not enough to do the whole assignments or duties scheduled for one working day, so increasing our productivity by using new techniques already created for that aim, will be our major topic to concentrate in this book. **Reaching your files** from any device from anywhere, will be your favorite option to do your job when and where is needed, by using the **MS OneDrive (Storage Cloud App)** built-in Windows 10, free of charge.

Time is so limited with every one of us nowadays, so all of us needs to get a good knowledge about something interesting with a very short period of time (**Fast Learning is the language of the century**), so in this case, you don't have to spend a lot of time studying this book as I made it short and simple to use, **so you may need only 5 to 6 hours to finish everything in details herein this book**.

Hint1: In this book, you will find the symbol "→" too much just to conclude the text needed for explanation. So, this symbol might mean (go to/ press on/ then/ click on, etc.). All this book is from my practical experience for a long 15 years with Microsoft Windows Operating Systems and for years with Windows 10 since its release until date.

Hint2: You will find no guide numbers for all screen snips, as you just need to be familiar with the most important windows, while the steps mentioned will guide you to reach your request and destination, easily with the icons and the step by step techniques.

Enjoy your learning journey…

"Knowing what to do & doing at well, is your biggest challenge at Work"

Let's overcome the whole Challenge

How to Get the Latest Updates for Windows 10?

To get the benefit of all new features in Windows 10, you have first to update your Windows 10

into the latest version that can be taken from the main website of Microsoft as follows:

- Before getting any updates that could be available on the main website of Microsoft, you

  have first to update your Windows 10 on your computer system in a regular procedure,

  so please head to ⊞ → ⚙ Settings → ↻ Update & Security → Check

  for Updates → if any updates are available → install them. Once you finish this step, then head

  into the next point.

- Now, to get the latest updates/ the latest version of windows 10, please go to

  https://www.microsoft.com/en-us/software-download/windows10, then `Update now`

  → `Run` → Click **Yes**, then follow the instructions until you finish updating your Windows 10

  into the latest version.

Download Windows 10

Windows 10 November 2019 Update

The Update Assistant can help you update to the latest version of Windows 10. To get started, click **Update now.**

`Update now`

Privacy

Create Windows 10 installation media

To get started, you will first need to have a license to install Windows 10. You can then download and run the media creation tool. For more information on how to use the tool, see the instructions below.

`Download tool now`

Privacy

Windows 10 Security and Account Protection

⠿ PIN   🔑 Password   ☺ Windows Hello

🖼 Picture password   Dynamic lock

Window 10 Security and Account Protection:

In Microsoft Windows 10, you will find the best security and account protection features/ options ever made by Microsoft, such as:

- Windows Account Password
- Window PIN Code
- Windows Hello
- Picture Password
- Windows Dynamic Lock

To get into the above features → ⊞ → ⚙ settings → ⧍ Accounts → ⚲ Sign-in options. Then you will see the first question on this screen (Sign-in Options) **"if you've been a way, when should Windows require you to sign in again?"** → When PC wakes up from sleep. Then you must **add** your **password** first and then you can add your **PIN Code** and **Picture** Password and set up your **Windows Hello** if your computer is compatible with the face recognition features. If your computer is not compatible with Windows Hello, you will notice a message telling you that under the Windows Hello option.

To set up **Windows Dynamic Lock,** go and make a ☑ tick mark and activate this option, to allow Windows to lock automatically your device when you are away. Then go to Bluetooth & other devices → click on Add Bluetooth or ＋ other device → then select ⚫ Bluetooth → then select your mobile device name → confirm connecting your devices.

 PIN  Password ☺ Windows Hello

 Picture password Dynamic lock

Cortana

App

How to get a personal digital assistant for you, **Cortana** will be your assistant everywhere you need her

Once you finish the next page, please go back here and try the followings:

Hay Cortana, "wake me up at nine o'clock"

Hay Cortana, "set a timer for 10 minutes"

Hay Cortana, "how is the weather today"

Hay Cortana, "what is the definition of livestock"

Hay Cortana, "how do you spell organization"

Hay Cortana, "how do you pronounce V, E, H, I, C, L, E"

Hay Cortana, "500+200+300 equals"

Hay Cortana, "shut down my PC"

Hay Cortana, "project my screen"

And so on…

◉ Cortana (Your Digital Personal Assistant):

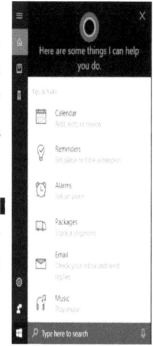

Cortana is one of the most important built-in applications in Windows 10, that can-do tons of things to you while you are at work or at home or even on the go 🧍. Its name came from "**Curtana**" which is the **Legendary Sword** ⚔ or a **Shortened Sword** (a **famous one belonged to an English King** ⚔) .

She is living and located on the left side of ⊞ ○ Type here to search 🎤 | Windows 10 Taskbar. Cortana can help you to increase your productivity and to avoid missing any of your business or personal issues, she can help you in the following fields / sectors:

Calendar	Finance
Reminders	Facts
Alarms	Math
Packages	Dictionary
Emails	Weather
Timers	News
Music	Chatting
Lists	Navigate your PC & Web
Search your stuff	Help with your PC
Places	Finance
Sports	& so many...

Note: you can call her for any help by saying "**Hay Cortana**", but that should be activated in advance. To activate her, go to Start Menu → Settings → Cortana → turn on "**Hay Cortana**", **keyboard shortcut** and **use Cortana even my device is locked** then click on check the microphone to make sure Cortana can hear you.

Alexa

App

Getting Alexa through Cortana will give you the power of both in one device

Once you finish the next page, please go back here and try the followings:

Hay Cortana, "open Alexa" once Alexa respond to you, say, "Alexa, do you hear me"

If you have smart home devices controlled by Alexa, you can try control them through your Windows 10 PC, just like that:

Hay Cortana, "open Alexa" once Alexa respond to you, say, "Alexa, turn on the bedroom lights"

If you want to install Alexa App from Microsoft Store, to deal with her without the need to call Cortana first, please head to Microsoft Store → search for Alexa → then install Alexa App → open it → sign-in by your Amazon account. Now you can activate ⌀ the Hands-free option by turn it on, then you can call Alexa directly just like that: **Alexa, "do you hear me"**.

Meet ⭕ Alexa (Your Digital Personal Assistant from Amazon) Through Cortana:

A great integration done between **Cortana** from **Microsoft** and **Alexa** from **Amazon**. By this way, you will be able to get the power of Alexa and Cortana in parallel on your MS Windows devices. From now on, you can control all of your smart home devices through this integration while you are at work or at home or even on the go 🧍. To get **Alexa** on your **Windows 10 laptop** for example, go and do left click on Cortana's search box on the taskbar → Say

"**Hay Cortana, open Alexa**" → then Cortana will say "First, sign in to Alexa" and she will open a Window → you must get-in the sign-in page from Amazon → enter your Amazon account that you already using on your Echo or Alexa enabled devices. Then follow the steps until you get Alexa on your Windows 10 device.

Important Note: If you want to get Alexa opened through your Cortana's Window, please call Cortana like that "**Hay Cortana, open Alexa**" in case you already activated the respond option "**Hay Cortana**" from Cortana's ⚙ settings, and Alexa will say immediately "**Hi, this is Alexa**". If you clicked on the **Mic** 🎤 that is located on the right side of Cortana's Search Box then you said "**open Alexa**" just like that, Cortana will try to open your **Alexa App** that is installed on your computer previously (in case you did it from Microsoft App Store). Once Alexa opened, you can ask her to do something with your smart home devices, such as turning off the living room lamp, etc...

You will notice that Alexa can't do everthing through Cortana because of the compatibility and other issues.

Windows Ink Workspace

Save the Earth, its environment and resources by using
Windows Ink Workspace options

New Windows Ink Workspace

Old Windows Ink Workspace

Windows Ink Workspace:

How to activate and show **Windows Ink Workspace Icon** on Window 10 Taskbar?

On any part of Windows 10 Taskbar (Part has no icon on it) → right click → **Show Windows Ink Workspace Button**, then the icon will be displayed on the right side of Windows 10 Taskbar.

To go paperless and to go green, you will find an excellent option on the Windows Ink Workspace area, called **(Sticky Notes)**.

Sticky Notes: Digital Sticky Notes will be an active sticky notes ready for your daily use instead of destroying the environment by using a huge number of paper sticky notes (Save the Earth, its environment and resources by using the available options in this area of Windows 10).

Hint1: Every person and every staff member can benefit a lot of these sticky notes as there is a **great integration** between the digital personal assistant (**Cortana**) and the information written on the sticky notes, in case we want to link it with **Cortana** for more help, as you will see it (the integration) on another part of this book. **Hint2:** In case the Windows Ink Workspace area doesn't match its picture on the right side, that means you have a newer version as you already saw it in previous page.

Sticky Notes

App

Every employee used to spend a lot of paper sticky notes every working day, can you imagine how many trees on the Earth being cut, to be transformed into a paper sticky notes ready for use at the workstation.

Can you imagine, if you could use a smart sticky notes (electronic), integrated with so many applications built-in Windows 10, and how much will help you to avoid missing any of your important issues

Sticky Notes (The Digital Sticky Notes and its integration with the other applications in Windows 10):

Sticky Notes is one of the most important options that you can go through it paperless, which is located in the 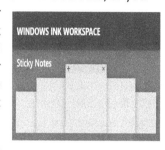 **Windows Ink Workspace area in the old version of Windows 10**, or you can find the Sticky Notes by searching for it on the search box available on the task bar area, that allows you to use a digital sticky notes synchronized on all of your windows devices, outlook, and anywhere else you sing-in by the same Microsoft email address.

There is a **great integration** between the digital personal assistant (**Cortana**) and the information written on the sticky notes, in case we want to link them with **Cortana**.

To activate and to open your sticky notes → 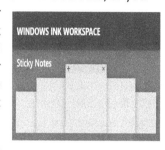 **Windows Ink Workspace** → Sticky Notes located on the top of Window Ink Workspace, if you couldn't find it because you have a newer version of Windows 10, then go to the search box and type Sticky Notes, then you will get into the welcome screen to the Sticky Notes.

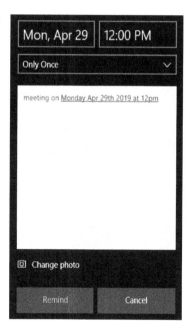

It is highly recommended to sign-in by your Microsoft email address, to get your sticky notes synced on all your Windows 10 devices and to be active and ready for use on Cortana. After that, you will get a Window for all the sticky notes created on your devices, in case you want to search for a specific one, you can do that through the same window. Try to right something on the yellow note area, 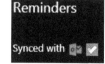 for example (**meeting on Monday Apr 29th 2019 at 12pm**), then your will notice that the date has been written in blue as a link, try to click on it, then click on **Add Reminder** and then click on **Remind.** Then you will link that note with **Cortana** to set a reminder with a message telling you that the note has been synced with your Outlook, as shown in the figures above.

"Whiteboard"

App

Every meeting, workshop and training session must have a white board ready for participants, to explain the major points or to share the whole ideas and problems with their solutions on it. But now, with Microsoft Whiteboard App, the online Whiteboard area will be an incredible option that can be used by a group of people from different places, who will be involved to explain their ideas for example on the same Whiteboard area.

Hint: To get the Whiteboard App installed in your computer, please head to the Windows Ink Workspace Icon 　　then open it → click on install Whiteboard, then you will get it installed and ready for use.

"Whiteboard" App:

Now with Windows 10, you can use and share a Whiteboard with

other colleagues to explain a matter or to have a session on a same

whiteboard for more collaboration online, with just a few clicks. Once you

need that Whiteboard, please head to the search box on the task bar → search for "**Whiteboard**"

App → open it → Click on Invite someone → then turn on Web sharing link → press on copy link

→ then send the copied link by email to the other colleagues to start the session on the

whiteboard, during the session, you can insert a picture, add a note, add a word document, add

PowerPoint document and so many things you can insert ⊞ from the insert menu button.

Once you have done, turn off the web sharing link then close the app. **Hint:** You may find the

Whiteboard icon available in the Windows Ink Workspace area, in case you have the updated

version of Windows 10.

Invite someone

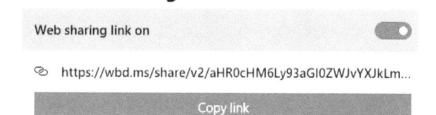

Create sharing link

Web sharing link on

https://wbd.ms/share/v2/aHR0cHM6Ly93aGl0ZWJvYXJkLm...

Copy link

Microsoft OneDrive

App

Increase your productivity by reaching your files from anywhere, from any device, anytime you need to, by using **MS OneDrive** in Windows10

Once you finish the next two pages, don't forget to go back to the below information

You may notice three signs/ icons under your documents stored in your OneDrive folder as follows:

Online-only

Online-only files don't take up space on this PC, and are downloaded as you use them.

Available on this device

Files with the green check mark are files that you already have downloaded and can be edited while you are offline.

Mark your important files

Ensure your important files are accessible by right clicking and choosing Always keep on this device

☁ Microsoft OneDrive:

In case you want to increase your productivity, you first have to reach your files from anywhere, from any device, anytime you need to, Microsoft **OneDrive** the Cloud Storage Built-in Application in Windows 10 has been located to make your dream comes true, so if you would like to activate this option in Windows 10 → [⊞] → [Recently added] → Left Click on "**O**" → then [☁ OneDrive] **OneDrive Setup Windows** will be displayed to start activating your OneDrive account by using one of your Microsoft Email accounts (**@outlook.com**, **@hotmail.com**, **@live.com**) → [Sign in] → Enter Email's Password → [Sign in] → [Next] → **Not now** if you want to get the **free 5GB Cloud Storage Space** ready for your use. Then the OneDrive icon [☁] will be displayed on the right side of Windows 10 Taskbar.

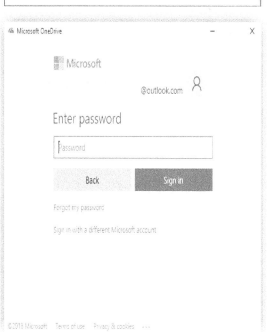

Online Microsoft OneDrive and Online Microsoft Office Applications

In case you don't have Microsoft Office Applications installed on your computer, the OneDrive webpage will give you the access to the most important Microsoft Office Applications, just by one click

Online Microsoft OneDrive and Online Microsoft Office Applications:

In case you want to reach your Microsoft OneDrive Online from your browser (Microsoft Edge, Chrome, Internet Explorer, etc.) → ⊞ → e → write https://onedrive.live.com → **Sign in** option located on the right upper side of the browser → right your Microsoft Email Account (@outlook.com, @hotmail.com, @live.com) → write your email's password → **sign in**, then your Online OneDrive account will be displayed with all of your files and folders.

Those who **doesn't have Microsoft Office applications**

installed on their own computers, they can benefit of the

online office applications that are available when they sign-

in to their **OneDrive account,** then go and press on the icon

⊞ → then all of Microsoft Online Office applications

will be ready for use without the need for any pre-

installation in advance, such as Microsoft **Word**, **Excel**,

PowerPoint, **OneNote**, etc.

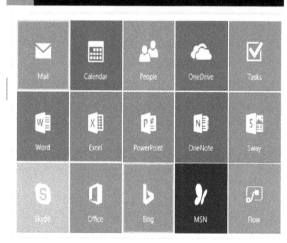

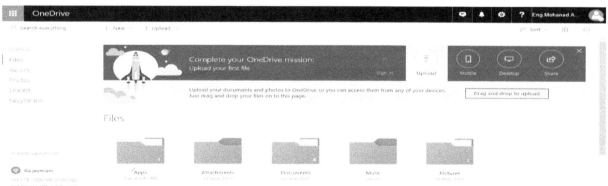

Windows Task View

Save your money and resources instead of buying many screens, by using **Windows Task View** option

Windows Multi-Tasking:

Task View option ⊡ (Old) or ⊟ (New) is one of the important options that is available in Windows 10, as you can open **multi-applications** on a **multi-Screens** at the same time, without the need to minimize the applications or to close some of them, just because you don't have enough space to view your applications at the same time on one screen.

So, if you would like to activate so many **desktop screens** at the same time → Task View Icon ⊡ (button) on Windows Taskbar → [+ New desktop] New Desktop button on the right side of the screen, then a new desktop will be displayed and ready to migrate your opened applications to it, by using the shortcut (⊞ + **Tab** button) on your keyboard → right click on one of the activated applications → move to → **desktop 2**. As shown below.

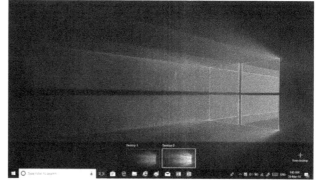

To switch between your screens in a professional way, you can use a great shortcut on your keyboard which is:

(**Ctrl** + ⊞ + **left** or **right arrows**)

To travel between your active screens in a very fast way. Enjoy your journey 🏂.

Quick Access to Files in Windows 10

Time is so limited with many of us, reaching a specific file with a very short time is the main technique in the next page

Quick Access to Files in Windows 10:

In regards on how to increase your productivity, there will be a great option available in Windows 10 that can be used to reach most of the files which were under editing recently on Microsoft Office applications as example, instead of searching for them in so many folders in different drives.

So, if you would like to activate this option → ⊞ → Right Click on Microsoft Word application icon → More → Pin to Taskbar, 📄 then a new icon will be displayed for Microsoft Word application on your Taskbar → Right Click on 📄 that icon on your Taskbar, then you will have a very quick access to your files edited 📄 recently on Microsoft Word.

Note: you can do that with the whole Microsoft Office applications and so many applications on your computer system.

ⓘ in some cases, and before having a **meeting** for example, you have to reach one of your edited files for that meeting to get a **printout** within a **moment**, so this option in Windows 10 will be your **favorite one at that time**, so Enjoooooy 🚀.

Touch Keyboard

Made for those who loved Emoticons or don't have a physical keyboard

Touch Keyboard with Emoticons 👲:

Windows Touch Keyboard is the great option for those who used to communicate using Emoticons, to express their messages with their feelings, so if you would like to activate this option in Windows 10, on any part of Windows 10 Taskbar (Part has no icon on it) → right click → **Show Touch Keyboard Button**, then the icon ⌨ will be displayed on the right side of Windows 10 Taskbar.

And to show the Touch Keyboard on your screen → ⌨ its Button on the right side of the Taskbar. Then you can enjoy with the Emoticons that are available in this option by clicking on 🙂 , then the whole Emoticons Buttons will be activated as shown below.

Note: you may notice some differences 🐷 when you get the emoticons on your documents or chatting areas, it will depend on the compatibility issues of the applications between each other. Now

Enjooooooy 🎢

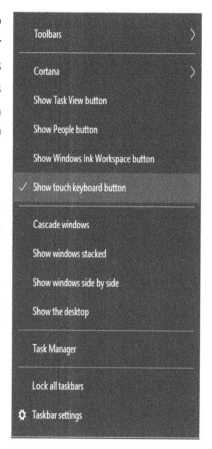

Action Center

People

Microsoft Store

Action Center, People and MS Store:

in Windows 10, you may notice some new icons on the Taskbar, such as

the [icon] **Action Center** icon, which can view all notifications you may

have on your computer system in this area.

Another important icon on your Taskbar will be for [icon] **Microsoft Store**,

in which you can find free and paid Applications, Music, Movies, Games, Books

and etc…

And the third icon you may see on your Taskbar, which will be the **People** [icon]

icon, through this icon you can **Pin** any of your **Contacts** you have on your

Skype and **Email**, this can be done if you already singed in Skype & Email with

your **Microsoft Account**.

In case you didn't find the People icon [icon] on the Taskbar → right click on

any empty area on the Taskbar → [Show People button] → then People icon will be displayed.

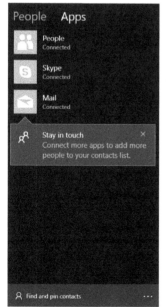

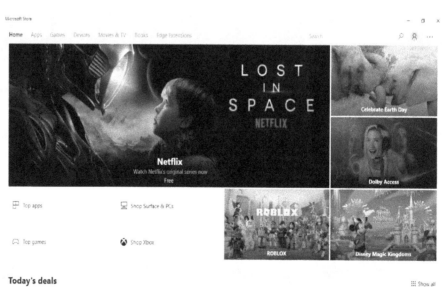

Start Menu

Personalize your **Start Menu** as much you can instead of full filling your Desktop to avoid affecting the computer's efficiency and slowing its speed

⊞ Start Menu (Personalizing Your Start Menu in Windows10):

To personalize your start menu in Windows 10 → ⊞ → right click on your program icon such as 🅆 MS Word → Pin to Start [📌 Pin to Start] → your program icon will be displayed on your Start Menu, then you can collect your preferred applications on a group of applications.

To group your applications in one place → left click and hold on your preferred application on the Start Menu → drag and drop the icons wherever is needed, then your applications will be grouped in one place on the Start Menu.

If you would like to rename your groups on your Start Menu → upper side of the group itself → give the

group a name such as (**Entertainment**) → press on **Enter Button**, then your group's name will be saved and displayed on the upper side of your applications group on the Start Menu.

<u>**Note:**</u> if you would like to move your group of applications from its place on the Start Menu to another place on it → left click and hold on the **group's name** itself → move the group to any place you want on the Start Menu → drop it on the preferred place, your group will be fixed on the new place you preferred.

Microsoft Edge

Microsoft Recommended Browser

Get tons of new features for **Microsoft Edge browser** built-in
Windows 10

Microsoft Edge Browser:

To get the benefit of all new features in Microsoft Edge browser that is built-in Windows 10, we will display some of the most useful features that can be used in the daily routine of your work on the web as follows:

- **Adding Extensions** that can be very helpful to you when you work on the web. Next page, you will see how to add extensions to the Edge browser.

- Instead of reading everything by yourself, let the **Microsoft Edge read everything** to you in **loud sound**. To get this option go to settings ••• then select A⁾ Read aloud Read Aloud.

- Opening **PDF files** on **Microsoft Edge** became more productive by adding **Notes**, **Highlights**, **sharing part of it**, **read it** all in loud sound (Female or Male Voice).

- **Ask Cortana**, your personal assistant could **enrich** your **search**, **information** and you may **save some money** with its suggestions. How to do that, just select what you need to ask for, then right click on your selection then click on **Ask Cortana about**...

- **Adding Notes** to any webpage you want, then share what you have mentioned and recommended on the webpage you made with your friends, colleagues and others, by using the share option. To find the both options, go to settings then more tools.

- Start your browsing on your phone, then continue on your Windows 10 PC and don't miss any of your searching details with Microsoft Edge on your Android and iOS devices. You will see how to do that in the next pages.

- **Reaching** your **favorite websites** from the **Taskbar**, by using **Pin This Page to the Taskbar** option that is available in Microsoft Edge. You can reach this option from settings menu.

Extensions for Microsoft Edge Browser

Empower your browser by having so many extensions free of charge

Microsoft Edge Extensions:

With Microsoft Edge browser, you can get a huge number of extensions specially made for it; that can be very helpful and useful during your work on this browser. To get the extensions: open the Microsoft Edge browser → ··· (Settings and More) → Extensions → Explore more extensions, then you will be able to install the extensions you want from Microsoft Store.

Some of the recommended extensions are as follows:

Translator that can translate websites into many languages

Translator for Microsoft Edge

Amazon Assistant

LastPass that can save your usernames and passwords

LastPass for Microsoft Edge

That can make your browser healthier for your eyes

Grammarly for Microsoft Edge

Turn Off the Lights™

Steps Recorder

App

Sometimes, you need to record your steps on your PC screen to explain something needed by someone else, **Steps Recorder** will be your best choice

Steps Recorder:

Steps Recorder option is one of the important options

that is available and built-in Windows 10, as you can

get the whole steps on your screen as screen shots

listed with some captions on a document, and then you

can take and edit the file, as you need, to be sent for

someone by email for example. This option can be your

favorite choice and the fastest one for this purpose.

So, if you would like to activate or to open the Steps

Recorder → Search box on Windows Taskbar → Type **Steps**

Recorder, then the app will be displayed → select it.

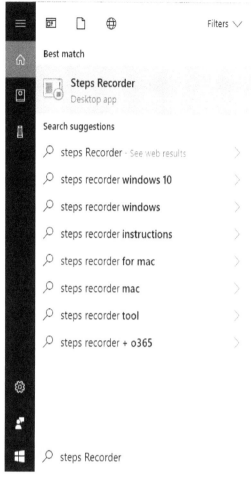

Then to start recording your steps on your screen press the Start Record Start Record Button.

Once you finish your required steps on the screen → Stop Record → Save → choose where

you want to save this file on your computer. Once you save the file, its format will be as a compressed file

(ZIP file format). You can open it on Microsoft Edge browser or any other ZIP file app reader. Instead of

getting too many print screens and saving one by one then editing them, **Steps Recorder can save your**

time and efforts.

Send to a PC

If you want to continue what you have on your mobile browser, and you would like to open it on your computer's browser, this option (**Send to a PC**) will be the best one for that mission.

Reflect Contents from Mobile Device to Windows 10 PCs by Using Microsoft Edge Browser:

If you would like to continue what you have on your [e] Mobile MS Edge Browser and to be opened and continued on your Windows 10 PC, there will be a great option available to do that, which is [→ send to a PC that is located in the middle of the Mobile MS Edge Browser.

First, you have to sign into the same Microsoft email account in both browsers, your Mobile and PC browsers. You can find the MS Edge Browser and get it free from the App or Play Store, then go to settings ··· → Sign in ⊗ → enter your MS email account and password. Then do the same with your MS Edge Browser on your PC. Once you done, open any website on your MS Mobile Edge Browser then click on [→ the send to a PC icon → select your PC from the Send to a [→ PC popup box, then you will get what you have on your mobile opened on your MS PC Edge Browser.

"Your Phone"

App

Getting your **photos**, **messages** and **notifications** from your phone displayed on your Windows 10 devices, will help you a lot to keep you updated and you will never miss anything important.
Try using "**Your Phone**" App

"Your Phone" App:

It is too important to get what you have on your phone such as the **messages**, **photos** and **notifications**, displayed on your Windows 10 devices, it's all about your productivity. Once you want to get that option (App made by MS Corporation) on your Windows 10 device, please head to the  MS Store → search for "**Your Phone**" App → Press on **Get** → once the App being installed → **Launch** → Type your phone # with the country code on the App, then follow the instructions and steps on both devices (Mobile and PC), to have your phone linked with your Windows 10 device. Don't forget to install the App "**Your Phone Companion**" on your mobile, to follow the steps on both devices in parallel.

"Quick Assist"

App

In case you have faced a problem with your Windows 10 PC, **Quick Assist App** will allow you to get the help from who will assess you remotely just by a few clicks, without the need to pre-install any other applications.

"Quick Assist" App:

Now with Windows 10, you can get a very quick assistant from another person who can help you to solve any problem on your personal computer with just a few clicks, you can share your screen with a full control on your computer by using the "**Quick Assist**" App that is built-in Windows 10. Once you need that assistant, please head to the search box on the task bar → search for "**Quick Assist**" App → open it → fill the box (the Code from assistant), but if you want to assist another person → Click on **Assist another person** → sing-in by your Microsoft account → give the code created by this app to whom you want to help to make him enter the code on his Quick Assist App. Then press on take full control of the remote computer then press continue to start the assistant. Once you finish, press on the stop button to stop the process, then close the App.

Security code: 071197
Code expires in **09:02**

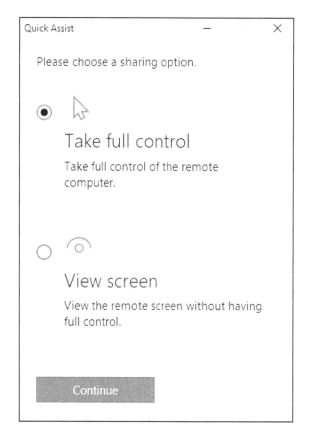

Mail App

Getting all your mail accounts tracked on one place, will be your favorite option to avoid missing any of your important matters

Mail App:

Most of the people have more than one email account, opening
them all through so many windows or tabs on browsers, will never
be effective like opening them all in one mailing application.

To get that option, please head to the search box on the taskbar and then write
"Mail" then open it → Add Account → select your account type → type your email address →
type your email's password → continue the steps until you finish setting up your mail account on
this App. Once you have done it, please repeat the whole steps to set up your second account as
you wish.

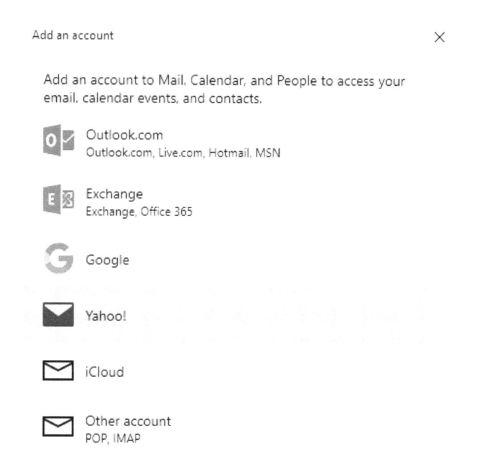

"Windows Logo Key" Keyboard Shortcuts -1

Press this key	To do this
Windows logo key + A	Open Action center.
Windows logo key + C	Open Cortana in listening mode. Notes • This shortcut is turned off by default. To turn it on, select **Start** > **Settings** > **Cortana**, and turn on the toggle under **Let Cortana listen for my commands when I press the Windows logo key + C**. Cortana is available only in certain countries/regions, and some Cortana features might not be available everywhere. If Cortana isn't available or is turned off, you can still use search.
Windows logo key + D	Display and hide the desktop.
Windows logo key + Alt + D	Display and hide the date and time on the desktop.
Windows logo key + E	Open File Explorer.
Windows logo key + L	Lock your PC or switch accounts.
Windows logo key + M	Minimize all windows.

Ref: https://support.microsoft.com/en-us/help/12445/windows-keyboard-shortcuts

"Windows Logo Key" Keyboard Shortcuts - 2

Press this key	To do this
Windows logo key + H	Start dictation.
Windows logo key + I	Open Settings.
Windows logo key + P	Choose a presentation display mode.
Windows logo key + Ctrl + Q	Open Quick Assist.
Windows logo key + S	Open search.
Windows logo key + Shift + S	Take a screenshot of part of your screen.
Windows logo key + T	Cycle through apps on the taskbar.
Windows logo key + period (.) or semicolon (;)	Open emoji panel.
Windows logo key + Tab Alt+ Tab	Open Task view. Shift between active apps
Windows logo key + Home	Minimize all except the active desktop window (restores all windows on second stroke).
Windows logo key + Spacebar	Switch input language and keyboard layout.
Windows logo key + Ctrl + Enter	Turn on Narrator.

Ref: https://support.microsoft.com/en-us/help/12445/windows-keyboard-shortcuts

Copy, Paste, And Other General Keyboard Shortcuts - 3

Press this key	To do this
Ctrl + X	Cut the selected item.
Ctrl + C (or Ctrl + Insert)	Copy the selected item.
Ctrl + V (or Shift + Insert)	Paste the selected item.
Ctrl + Z	Undo an action.
Alt + Tab	Switch between open apps.
Alt + F4	Close the active item, or exit the active app.
Windows logo key + L	Lock your PC.
Windows logo key + D	Display and hide the desktop.
F2	Rename the selected item.
F3	Search for a file or folder in File Explorer.
F4	Display the address bar list in File Explorer.
Ctrl + X	Cut the selected item.

Ref: https://support.microsoft.com/en-us/help/12445/windows-keyboard-shortcuts

Copy, Paste, And Other General Keyboard Shortcuts - 4

Press this key	To do this
Ctrl + X	Cut the selected item.
Ctrl + C (or Ctrl + Insert)	Copy the selected item.
Ctrl + V (or Shift + Insert)	Paste the selected item.
Ctrl + Z	Undo an action.
Alt + Tab	Switch between open apps.
Alt + F4	Close the active item, or exit the active app.
Windows logo key + L	Lock your PC.
Windows logo key + D	Display and hide the desktop.
F2	Rename the selected item.
F3	Search for a file or folder in File Explorer.
F4	Display the address bar list in File Explorer.
Ctrl + X	Cut the selected item.

Ref: https://support.microsoft.com/en-us/help/12445/windows-keyboard-shortcuts

Copy, Paste, And Other General Keyboard Shortcuts - 5

Press this key	To do this
F5	F5
Refresh the active window.	Refresh the active window.
Ctrl + A	Ctrl + A
Select all items in a document or window.	Select all items in a document or window.
Ctrl + D (or Delete)	Ctrl + D (or Delete)
Delete the selected item and move it to the Recycle Bin.	Delete the selected item and move it to the Recycle Bin.
Ctrl + R (or F5)	Ctrl + R (or F5)
Refresh the active window.	Refresh the active window.
Ctrl + Y	Ctrl + Y
Redo an action.	Redo an action.
Ctrl + Alt + Tab	Ctrl + Alt + Tab
Use the arrow keys to switch between all open apps.	Use the arrow keys to switch between all open apps.

Ref: https://support.microsoft.com/en-us/help/12445/windows-keyboard-shortcuts

How to Increase Your Computer's Speed from 15 to 35 Times More than Normal

Now a days, you can upgrade your old desktop PC or laptop to be a very fast computer system, just by replacing one item in your PC, which is the Hard Disk Drive (HHD) into a <u>Solid State Drive (SSD), which has 15 to 35 times faster</u> than the HHD. Windows 10 can be very fast and very responsive with everything installed on the SSD with unexpected speed of performance (**incredible performance**). If would like to try that, please ask an IT man or office to check and to make sure that your computer is compatible to get the SSD. For your information, if you have a limited budget and you already have your work stored on a cloud, in this case you don't have to buy a high storage capacity, you just need to speed up your computer performance with one of the (SSD) editions. You will find a lot of choices matched with your available budget.

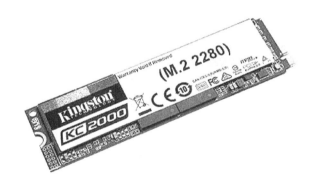

Last Advice

To complete your capacity development, you must continue practicing on

Microsoft Office Applications specially **Word**, **Excel**, **PowerPoint**, **Outlook** and

OneNote, then you must teach yourself **fast typing** on the keyboard, <u>**without the**</u>

<u>**need to look at it**</u>. Please try to search the web for the free typing software,

websites and lessons. In that way, you will **increase your productivity 100%** more

than before.

Wish you a Good Luck

Coming Next

Alexa

The Teacher

How to make your children overcome most of their challenges at school by making them study with

Amazon Alexa

with a high level of

Motivation